the parent's Helping Hand Book

a practical guide for teaching your child Protective Behaviours

by Holly-ann Martin

The Parent's Helping Hand Book
by Holly-ann Martin

First published November 2007
by Protecting Kids is Our Game

2nd Publication May 2009
by Monarch Publishing House Pty Ltd

3rd Publication January 2012
by Safe4Kids Pty Ltd
www.safe4kids.com.au
PO Box 367
Armadale WA 6992
Australia
©2012 Safe4Kids

Printed by CreateSpace, an Amazon.com Company

This publication contains the opinions and ideas of its author. It is intended to provide helpful and informative material on the subject matter covered. It is not intended to replace professional services and is given in good faith for the purpose of raising awareness and in an advisory capacity only.

Every effort has been taken to make this book as complete and accurate as possible.
Whilst written in good faith, the author and publisher assume no responsibility for any liability, loss, or risk, personal or otherwise, which is incurred as a consequence, directly or indirectly, of the use and application of any of the contents of this book.

All rights reserved. No part of this book may be reproduced, stored in a retrieval system or transmitted by any means, eg; mechanical, electronic, photocopying, recording or otherwise, without written permission from the author, for reasons other than teaching your child, or children, Protective Behaviours.

Illustrations by Marilyn Fahie
Cover designed by Tracey Gibbs
Edited by Jane Bracho

National Library Australia
Cataloguing-in-Publication Data

ISBN 978-0-9803240-9-9

Martin, Holly-ann
The Parent's Helping Hand Book: A practical guide for teaching your child Protective Behaviours.

© Copyright 2012 safe4kids

Contents

Introduction	1
Foreword	2
Theme 1: We all have the right to feel safe all of the time.	3
Feelings	4
The Safety Continuum	7
Early Warning Signs	9
Theme 2: We can talk with someone about anything.	13
Networks	13
Persistence	16
Public and Private	17
Strangers	18
Personal Space	19
The Three Safety Questions	19
Secrets	21
Secret Enablers	23
It's ok for children to say "No" to adults	24
Cyber Safety	25
Cyber Agreement	26
Other things to consider	27
Receiving a Disclosure	28

© Copyright 2012 safe4kids

Introduction

Teaching your children Protective Behaviours can be one of the most challenging aspects of parenting. How do you prepare them for the potential dangers that exist in the world without scaring them, wrapping them in cotton wool, or providing 'too much information'?

It's a sensitive issue.

You may find some of the information contained in this booklet confronting, so use your discretion. You may wish to use your own examples of what you consider age appropriate for your child. However, this book provides a holistic approach to teaching Protective Behaviours and so it is important that you teach all the lessons, teach everything in sequence, and leave nothing out.

Teaching your children the language and principles of Protective Behaviours as young as possible can help protect them from potential harm as well as provide them with invaluable life skills.

It is never too early or too late to teach children Protective Behaviours.

Starting as early as possible provides many wonderful opportunities for 'teachable moments.' For example, in day to day situations such as bathing or dressing, reading picture books, going to new places, meeting new people or watching television there is a wealth of teachable moments.

The Parent's Helping Hand Book is based on the themes, core concepts and strategies of the Protective Behaviours Program designed by Peg Flandreau West. This program has been adapted, expanded upon and refined to produce the Safe4Kids Program©

Foreword

I can not begin to express the impact the Protective Behaviours program has had on my life as an adult. I am extremely grateful that I was able to witness the program being taught in my classroom and wish that I had been exposed to the program as a child.

When I was young I was sexually abused by a family 'friend'. Later, as a teenager I was sexually assaulted by a man who is a health professional. The Protective Behaviours program empowered me to trust my own instincts about what had happened to me and finally report the sexual assault to police.

By watching the Protective Behaviours program being taught in my classroom I learnt many concepts that, upon reflection, have helped me understand that I was not responsible for what happened to me. The concepts of public and private places, public and private body parts, the importance of persistence, Early Warning Signs, good and bad secrets and having a Network of trusted adults are all important concepts that, if I had known them, may have helped protect me from sexual abuse. If only I'd known about the importance of persistence, telling and telling and telling people about things that bothered me until someone paid attention and, most importantly, validated that what had happened to me was wrong then I would have been able to free myself from the pain, shame and guilt earlier in my life.

I can't stress enough the importance of children needing to understand that their bodies belong to them and that they have a right to feel safe all of the time. Most children are taught that adults have the final word, but unfortunately not all adults are trustworthy or have children's best interest at heart.

Protective Behaviours empowers children to protect themselves. Yes, the program can be confronting for adults. Nobody wants to think about children being sexually abused, especially because in most cases the perpetrator is someone the child knows. But this attitude only protects the perpetrators. The Protective Behaviours program needs to be taught to all children and I will most definitely be teaching my son Protective Behaviours concepts, as soon as he is old enough to understand.

Carla Hampton
School Teacher & Mother

Theme 1:
We all have the right to feel safe all of the time.

Unpack Theme One:

- Discuss who we mean when we say, 'We'. We mean everyone; even 'bullies', 'baddies' and 'robbers' have the right to feel safe. They may have made bad choices but they still have the right to feel safe.
- Discuss what a 'Right' is… it is a human right, you are born with it, it doesn't have to be earned and no-one can take it away from you. It's like the right to have food, clothing, shelter and education.
- Discuss that with Rights come Responsibilities. If you have the right to feel safe, you also have a responsibility to not make others feel unsafe.
- Discuss what it feels like to feel 'Safe'
- List words that mean the same as safe; secure, loved, warm, cosy, protected and cared for.
- Discuss what it feels like to feel 'Unsafe'.
- What happens in our bodies when we feel unsafe? List words that mean the same as unsafe; danger, under threat, intimidated, frightened, afraid, worried and feeling not cared for.
- Discuss the differences between feeling safe and being safe. In a thunderstorm, you may be safe inside your home but the loud noise may make you feel unsafe.
- Discuss what 'all of the time' means. At school, in the playground, at home, at the shops, in the cinema, when you are away on camp, visiting friends or anywhere else. You have the right to feel safe everywhere, all of the time, and if you don't that is why you need to know Protective Behaviours.

- » A child might feel unsafe about getting into trouble. Discuss the difference between getting into trouble for doing something wrong, and feeling unsafe, scared or hurt. Make sure they understand that you may not like their behaviour and that's why they are in trouble, but you still love them and they still have the right to feel safe.
- » Road and water safety may be a good starting point for discussing Safety.
- » Use the word 'Safe' as part of your family's everyday conversation.
- » Encourage your child to feel confident about expressing feelings openly. A child who is told, "Stop crying!", "Don't be silly," or "Don't be scared," will learn that their feelings don't matter or are not valid.

HANDY HINTS

Feelings

'Yes' feelings and 'No' feelings / 'Safe' and 'Unsafe' feelings / 'Comfortable' and 'Uncomfortable' feelings.

It is important to teach children the names of emotions so that they can express how they are feeling. Encourage them to express how they are feeling, especially when they have a dispute, so that they can use their words instead of making bad choices with their actions. Also, encourage your child to use their words if someone hits them rather than hitting them back. Say, "Stop it. I don't like it when you hit me, it makes me feel ..." Or if they are being stared at say, "Stop it. I don't like it when you stare at me, it makes me feel ..."

As adults, we need to accept how children feel and avoid discounting their feelings, avoid telling a child that they are being silly if they feel scared during a thunderstorm or are afraid of the dark. Encourage them to think of ways that they could problem solve the situation and help make themselves feel safe again.

Discuss with your child how some touches can give you 'Yes' feelings or 'No' feelings. For example, a cuddle may be a 'Yes' feeling and a pinch or a bite would be a 'No' feeling. Feelings can differ from person to person, for example, some people like to be tickled and some don't. Discuss with family members about listening to your child if they don't like to be tickled. Nobody can tell you how you feel. Avoid making children kiss adults, if your child doesn't want to kiss someone ask them why. It does not matter if their reason makes no sense to you, if it is traumatic for the child that is your guideline.

 Complete the worksheet you consider age appropriate for your child from the two sheets on the following pages and encourage discussion about their feelings in each situation on that sheet.

» Model speaking about your own feelings to your children, whether good or bad.
» Children need to understand that they are not allowed to make you feel unsafe either. For instance, when your child asks to sleep over at a friend's house and you are not keen on the idea, please don't say to your child, "Because I said so!" as a reason for not allowing them to go. Explain why you don't feel safe about them sleeping over, without giving specific information that may scare them. Explaining will save many family arguments, and teach children that they can rely on your judgment.

HANDY HINTS

Feelings

Have your child answer each of these questions as part of a game.

How would you feel

if someone was
hurting you?

if your Mum was
reading you a bedtime story?

if you lost your
favourite toy?

in a thunderstorm?

 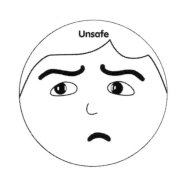

if someone was taking
your lunch money?

sitting on a parent's
lap having a cuddle?

© Copyright 2012 safe4kids

Feelings

Have your child answer each of these questions as part of a game.

How would you feel

the night before a big
event or a party?

on a wet afternoon in the holidays?

standing up and speaking at
the school assembly?

if your little sister was
getting all the attention?

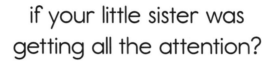

if an older child was taking
your lunch money?

if you started at a new school?

if you kept trying to do
something but just couldn't do it?

if your little brother kept coming into
your room and breaking things?

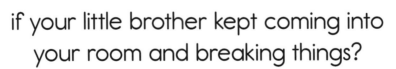

if you were picked
as the captain of a sports team?

if someone was hurting you?

© Copyright 2012 safe4kids 6

Safety Continuum

Safe - Fun to Feel Scared - Risking on Purpose - Unsafe

⟵⟶

Safety = Choice + Control + Time Limit

Children need to be encouraged to be adventurous, in a positive and informed way. They need to be able to make good choices as you will not always be there to protect them or help them make their choices.

The Safety Continuum teaches children that to feel safe you need to have a choice, have some kind of control or have a time limit on the event or activity.

Discuss the difference between positive, healthy risk taking (Risking on Purpose) and reckless, unsafe or destructive behaviour.

Safety is an emotional, psychological and physical state, so discuss with your child that to feel safe there must be choice or control and/or a time limit.

» Adolescents may tend to put themselves at risk in unsafe situations, due to peer pressure, drug taking and other outside influences. Teach them the difference between Risking on Purpose and reckless or unsafe behaviours – and reinforce that they can come to you and talk about 'anything' – this 'backup' will give them confidence and help them make safer choices.

» Talk with them about how they are feeling and the pressure they are under for acceptance and what they can do about things that make them feel pressured.

» I recommend reading 'Too safe for their own good.' How risk and responsibility help teens thrive, by Michael Ungar, PhD.

HANDY HINTS

Safe:

The experience of safety may differ from person to person so explore with your child what makes them feel secure and protected. Discuss with your child how in some situations you can start off feeling safe but the situation can escalate into feeling unsafe. For example, being tickled can start off being funny and pleasurable and end up with you feeling like you are going to wet your pants. For older children discuss how kissing and petting may lead to being pressured into going further.

Fun to feel scared:

Sometimes it's fun to feel scared. It can be exciting or an adventure with a focus on fun. You may get your Early Warning Signs, but you are in control, you have a choice or there is a time limit on the activity. For example, when going on a ride at the show, you have a choice about going on the ride, you may not be in control, but you know that after a short time the ride will end.

Risking on Purpose:

Is about taking calculated risks to help you reach your goals. You deliberately choose to take certain risks to get better at or learn certain things. Sometimes you have to take risks or there may be a negative outcome. Some examples of Risking on Purpose: having an injection, trying new food, going to the dentist, learning to ride a bike. Again, the criteria is choice, control and time limit. For example, when having a needle, you may feel scared, you may not have a choice about it or may not be in control, but you know after the initial pain of the needle going in, it will all be over very quickly.

Unsafe:

Feeling unsafe may also differ from person to person so explore with your child what makes them feel threatened, insecure and unprotected. Discuss with your child how you can start off feeling unsafe in a situation and continue down the continuum ending in feeling safe; for example learning to ride a bike, learning to swim etc. Because you risked on purpose and persisted you begin to feel safe in that situation. This can be a good time to tell your children what sort of things make *you* feel insecure or unprotected, being mindful not to burden them with personal issues.

© Copyright 2012 safe4kids

Early Warning Signs

Early Warning Signs are involuntary physical sensations which our bodies feel when we do not feel safe, when we are excited or when we are in challenging situations. It is our natural 'fight or flight' response to perceived danger.

Each individual is different, therefore it is important to provide children with a chance to experience their Early Warning Signs in a controlled situation so they can learn to identify them. Help your child to learn to identify their Early Warning Signs by supervising them in one or more of the following activities:

- Walk on a balance beam
- Wear a blindfold
- Blow up and burst a balloon
- Try a visualisation
- Watch a popup toaster
- Make popcorn
- Go on play equipment that is high up
- Watch a jack-in-the-box
- Carry a bucket of water and don't spill any
- Listen to music that builds to a climax

Discuss the different sensations that the children experience and have them draw a pictorial representation of what they think this looks like on a body outline (see pages 11-12)

Dobbing vs Telling:

» Once children understand about their Early Warning Signs it is an opportune time to teach the difference between Dobbing and Telling.

» If you are Dobbing you are trying to get someone in trouble.

» If you are Telling you will have your Early Warning Signs, you may feel unsafe, you may have concerns about yourself or someone else, so you must tell someone you trust.

» Once your children have this fully explained to them they will be able to understand the difference between Dobbing and Telling. Empower them to distinguish if they are Dobbing or Telling when they are telling you something by asking them if they are getting their Early Warning Signs, do they feel unsafe? Or are they just trying to get that person in trouble?

HANDY HINTS

Early Warning Signs

I get my early warning signs when I feel unsafe

If I get my Early Warning Signs I must keep telling an adult I trust until I feel safe again.

Early Warning Signs

I get my early warning signs when I feel unsafe

If I get my Early Warning Signs I must keep telling an adult I trust until I feel safe again.

Theme 2:
"We can talk with someone about anything."

Unpack Theme Two:

- Discuss who we mean when we say 'We'. We mean everyone.
- Discuss who the someone could be.
- Discuss what anything could be; if it's unsafe, awful, yucky, nasty, rude or unwanted touching, or something fun, pleasurable and exciting.

Networks

Help your children to develop a Network of trusted adults who will provide support and protect them if necessary.

The criteria for being a Network person is an adult who will:

1. ...listen.
2. ...believe them.
3. ...be available and accessible.
4. ...take action, if necessary, to protect them and help them feel safe again.

Complete the Network worksheet (see over page) using the thumb for an adult who lives in your home, second and third fingers for school staff, and the fourth and fifth fingers for family or community members not living in the same home. For example, another parent (if not living in home), grandparent, neighbour, aunts, uncles or adults at out of school activities (eg; sports coach, scout leader), parents of friends, church leaders, family doctor, etc.

Your child may wish to place friends, siblings, pets, toys etc on their palm – these are not Network people but they may choose to practice telling them about what is upsetting them. Encourage your child to go with a friend or take the toy to tell a Network person when they are feeling unsafe.

Use the wrist for an Emergency Network including Police (000) Security Guards or Shop Keepers (if they are lost), Duty Teachers and Kids Helpline 1800 551 800 (Australia only).

- Display your child's Network with names and contact phone numbers in your home.
- Teach your child their own address and phone number, how to use the phone, how to ring 000 and practice answering the phone. Also teach them what to say on the phone if you are not home, which in most instances does not include giving out personal information to who is on the other end.
- An Emergency is when you need help urgently, quickly, straight away. Discuss with your child how in emergencies it is ok to break the rules. For example, if you go to the shops with a parent of the opposite sex, it is ok to use the disabled toilets in an emergency so that the parent can check to make sure the toilet is empty/safe, and then wait for you directly outside. Normally you would not be able to use the disabled toilets unless you have a disability. This is breaking the rules to stay safe.
- Avoid saying to children that the police will get them if they don't behave, if you use this as a threat it creates fear about police and may discourage your child from seeking help from a police officer.
- Encourage your child to share good news, like receiving an award or achieving good test results, with their Network people as this ensures that the lines of communication are already there.
- Practice talking with your children about what is happening in their lives. Show them that you will listen to anything they have to say especially if they are experiencing difficult or embarrassing issues, or even if they have done something wrong. Make sure they understand that no matter what they have done, you may not like the behaviour, it may be something they will get in trouble for, but you still love them. Reassure them that you're glad they told you to ensure you always keep the communication lines open.
- 'Talk Soon. Talk Often'. This is a great free resource which guides parents in the conversation with their kids about sex and sexual matters. It can be found at ... http://www.public.health.wa.gov.au/2/1276/2/parentcaregiver.pm
- Reassure your child that you will always listen and believe them and that they can tell you anything.

HANDY HINTS

We can talk with someone about anything

My Network

These are people I can trust when I don't feel safe.
If I get Early Warning Signs I can talk with them.

They will listen to me.

They will believe me.

They are available.

They will take action if
necessary.

Kids Help Line
1800 551 800

15 © Copyright 2012 safe4kids

Review Networks:

> » Encourage your child to review their Network regularly as it gives them a chance to assess whether all the people on their Network are appropriate and up to the task. Just before the school holidays is an opportune time for this review as your child may not have access to school staff over the holiday period.

Adolescents:

> » Peers may offer unconditional friendship and support but it's important that adolescents feel they can also tell an adult about their fears to ensure they get appropriate help to feel safe. Talk with them about how they are feeling and the pressure they are under for acceptance. Discuss what forms this takes, and what they can do about it.

> » Separate your child's actions from their behaviour. For example, if they are suspended from school would this be the worst thing they would ever have to tell you? Remember, you want to reinforce the second theme of Protective Behaviours that they can talk with someone about anything. Children sometimes refrain from seeking help because they are afraid of the consequences; some children put up with SMS bullying because they believe their parents will confiscate their mobile phones.

HANDY HINTS

Persistence

Persistence is a crucial strategy of Protective Behaviours as a child may not be believed or may still have their Early Warning Signs after telling an adult that they feel unsafe. You must encourage your children to keep on telling, keep on telling until they feel safe or until their Early Warning Signs go away.

Encourage them to persist in all aspects of their lives, including not giving up when they are trying something new, when Risking on Purpose, if they are getting into trouble for something they didn't do, or if they don't understand instructions. The only way to bring about change in any of these circumstances is through persistence.

Public and Private

Public means people around. Private means just for you.

It is very important that your child be taught the correct names for their private body parts and that private means just for them. Private body parts are those parts of the body that are covered by bathers and also include the mouth. Reinforce with your child that they own the whole of their body and no-one should touch any part of them unless they give permission.

Teaching Public and Private as a whole concept rather than just focusing on body parts makes it less embarrassing.

Public and Private rooms and places:

Private rooms in your home are bathrooms, bedrooms and toilets. These are private rooms because we practice private behaviours when we are alone in them. Closing the door makes the rooms private. A private place is only private when you are alone in it.

Note: Explain to and discuss with your child that the internet is a public place.

Public and Private behaviours and body functions:

Behaviours such as nose-picking, burping, spitting, passing wind, swearing, etc are private and should be conducted in private. You may also want to teach your child that what happens at home is private, and if they are feeling unsafe about something happening in their home they may tell somebody on their Network, but they shouldn't share it with their class for Show and Tell. Network people will understand and respect their privacy unless they get their own Early Warning Signs, then they may have to use their own Network.

Public and Private clothing:

Private clothing is clothing that directly covers your private body parts and is worn underneath public clothes. Swimming clothes also cover private body parts but do not have to be covered by public clothes while you are using them.

Public and Private body parts:

Private body parts include bottom, breasts, penis, vagina and mouth. Ensure your child has a clear understanding that Private means just for them and they are the only ones that can touch their private parts. If it is necessary for someone, for example, a doctor, dentist or parent to examine their private body parts, those people must ask permission first, and have an explanation for why the examination is necessary.

HANDY HINTS

» Bath or dressing time is a great time for teaching Public and Private because you are teaching it in familiar and comfortable situations.

» Teach your child that if they are feeling unsafe it is important that they speak with someone on their Network privately rather than disclosing in public.

» It is not enough to just teach your child Early Warning Signs to protect them from unwanted touching, by teaching Public and Private it gives them a clear rule that nobody is allowed to touch their private body parts without their permission, and it also teaches them in which instances they would need to give their permission.

Strangers

Ask your child to describe their perception of a stranger. Common answers from children are that they are bad people, they are only men, they are robbers and criminals, etc.

We take for granted that children know what a stranger is, but this is a concept we need to teach them.

A stranger is a person you don't know.

You can't tell by looking at a stranger if they are safe person or an unsafe person. It's not about scaring children about strangers, because sometimes in an emergency it may be a stranger that will help them. For example, if they are lost they may need to ask a passerby for directions or assistance – but children need to be taught to be wary.

In case your child becomes lost teach them to look for a stranger wearing a badge, like a shopkeeper, a police officer or a security guard, as they have a purpose for being there and a duty of care. If there is no-one wearing a badge then a lady with a pram or with children may be the next best person to ask for help.

Teach your child that they should never leave a shop with a stranger, never take food or money from a stranger and never, ever get into a car with a stranger, no matter what this person says or promises, even if he says he has instructions from the child's parents.

© Copyright 2012 safe4kids **18**

Note: Discuss strangers on the internet with your children and teens. It is especially difficult for young people to understand that people may not be who they say they are when they present themselves on the internet, and that even adults have no way of finding out exactly who anyone is on the internet.

Personal Space

Teach children that they are the most important person in their life and that the space around them belongs to them. It is called their 'Personal Space', and they have a right to defend it. If somebody is standing too close they have the right to say, "Excuse me, you are standing in my personal space." They have a right to say who can touch, hug and kiss them. Talk to your family members about hugging and kissing, tell them that your child may not want to hug or kiss them sometimes or at all, and that this is ok.

Children need to know that you will protect and defend them. If you haven't clearly given them this message, they will assume that they have to always do what an adult wants them to do, and that you may side against them with another adult.

Three Safety Questions

1. Do I get a 'yes' or a 'no' feeling?

2. Does an adult I live with know where I am?

3. Can I get help if I need it?

The aim of teaching the Three Safety Questions is to encourage children to ask these questions of themselves before doing something that is unsafe, Risking on Purpose or going with someone that they may or may not know. For example, a child may go to a friend's house, their parent knows they are at the friend's house but what would they do if a neighbour asked them to go to the pool with her family for a swim? The child needs to stop and ask the Three Safety Questions. They may get a yes feeling, but does an adult they live with know where they are? What if there is an emergency – would their parent know where to find them? You may want to use a relevant story from the news as an example to teach them the necessity of having their caregivers always know where they are, but do not use frightening imagery.

In any given situation, if your child asks the Three Safety Questions and answers 'no' to any of them, they need to stop and problem solve. For example, if an adult they live with does not know where they are, and they wanted to go to the pool with the neighbour, they could make a phone call and get permission. Brainstorm other solutions with your child.

Enlarge the worksheet below and create a poster. Have your child draw pictures that will help them remember the Three Safety Questions. You can keep all of the worksheets completed in Protective Behaviours in a special file or box and placed in a special place in your home, so your child always knows where his or her helpful information is kept.

Three Safety Questions

1. Do I get a 'Yes' or a 'No' feeling?

1 | yes | no |

2. Does an adult I live with know where I am?

2

3. Can I get help if I need it?

3

© Copyright 2012 safe4kids **20**

Secrets

Discuss with your child the difference between

Good/Safe/Comfortable Secrets
and
Bad/Unsafe/Uncomfortable Secrets

A Good Secret will make somebody feel happy when it is revealed, and it is usually only kept for just a short time.

A Bad Secret will make somebody feel unsafe and they will be told they must never tell or that the secret must be kept for a lifetime. Teach your child that they must never keep Bad Secrets. Other ways children can identify a Bad Secret is that there may only be two people that know the secret, or it may give them their Early Warning Signs.

Teach your child that they should never have to keep secrets about any kind of touching and that they should always tell somebody on their Network if someone asks them to keep a Bad Secret of any kind.

Use the worksheet adjacent to help reinforce examples of Good and Bad Secrets. Come up with ideas of your own. Ask your child to join in and give examples of good or bad secrets. Sometimes they get confused about the difference, and this is a good time to correct it.

» Have a secret family password, a code word for emergencies, so that if anyone is sent to unexpectedly pick your child up from school etc, they must know the password. It could also be useful if you are out at a party, busy doing something or in a public place and your child needs to get your attention straight away. It needs to be a word or phrase that only the family members know, it is not to be shared with anyone else unless in an emergency.

» Have a secret family telephone ring code so your child can let you know they have arrived safely; ring twice, hang up, ring twice again, or ring three times and hang up, etc.

» In case your child comes home and you are not at home, have a secret key hidden somewhere outside so they can get into the house. Do not hide it in a place where people would ordinarily look. Make sure that everyone in the family, and only family members, know where the key is kept.

HANDY HINTS

Secrets

It is fun to keep a Secret, you might feel excited about keeping a Secret. But there are two different kinds of Secrets:

Good/Safe/Comfortable Secrets

and Bad/Unsafe/Uncomfortable Secrets

A good Secret is like a surprise. It will make someone feel happy and you only have to keep the Secret for a short time.

A bad Secret will make you feel uncomfortable and unsafe. It is a Secret that may give you your Early Warning Signs and the person who tells you the Secret will want you to keep the Secret for a long time, or even for a life time. Never keep a bad Secret or Secret about any type of touching, always tell someone on your Network, and remember that if the first or even second person is not listening, keep telling till someone does listen.

Read these Secrets and colour the Good/Safe/Comfortable Secrets in Green and the Bad/Unsafe/Uncomfortable Secrets in Red.

1.   Where presents are hidden.
2.   You saw someone steal something.
3.   Someone is taking your lunch money from you.
4.   What you made your Dad for Father's Day.
5.   Where your family hide their spare key.
6.   Your sister has a secret friend on the internet.
7.   Your Mum's surprise birthday party.
8.   Someone is hurting you.
9.   Where you hide your box of treasures.
10. Someone tried to touch your Private Parts.

© Copyright 2012 safe4kids

Secret Enablers

Perpetrators employ strategies to get children to keep a secret. Talk about the words below and what they mean to help your children understand what sort of things might be used to get their agreement to keep a secret. Remind them about Theme Two and let them know that you will always believe them and do your best to protect them from harm. The examples given below are for your benefit; please use your own judgment about using these examples for your children. Use your own examples if you find it necessary.

Tricks: This means something you do to deceive or cheat somebody. An example is - "Let's play this little game. Only you and I can play it."

Threat: This means a warning that something unpleasant, future harm, punishment or danger may happen. An example of a threat is - "If you tell anyone about this they will put you into a children's home and you will never see your parents ever again."

Bribe: This is a treat, a gift, or money given to somebody to make them to do something illegal, unlawful, unwanted, wrong or dishonest. An example is - "I'll buy you a play station if you promise not to tell."

Blackmail: Is the crime of trying to get something from someone by threatening to reveal a secret that they don't want other people to know about. Payment made to stop information that could bring shame or disgrace. An example might be - "You have done it before, so you have to do it again. If you don't I'll tell all your friends and they will know how disgusting you are."

Lies: Are something that is said that is untrue. Someone might say - "Adults don't believe what children say,"

Guilt: Is the feeling you get when you have done something wrong or committed a crime. An example is - "You did that, and you will be in big trouble if people find out." Someone may use your guilt over something you have done to get you to do things you do not want to do.

Shame: Is a painful feeling of having lost the respect of others because of improper or unwise behaviour which brings dishonor or disgrace to themselves or their family. A feeling of guilt or embarrassment. You may be manipulated by - "If you tell anyone what we are doing, everyone will know what a bad person you are and all your friends and family will never talk to you again."

Conning: Is being sucked in by something, being betrayed, tricked or conned. Someone might say – that they are from a modeling company and if you send them money for photos they will sign you up for a modeling contract.

It's ok for children to say "No" to adults.

Teach your child it is ok to say "no" to anyone, including adults, if they are getting their Early Warning Signs and feeling unsafe.

Explain to your child that if an adult tells them to eat their vegetables or go to bed then they have to do as they are told as this doesn't make them feel unsafe. They may not like their veggies, but veggies don't give them their Early Warning Signs.

But if **anyone** tells them to do something that is unsafe, touches their private body parts or does anything that gives them their Early Warning Signs, they don't have to obey - they can say "No!", and even if they are threatened someone on their Network will help them deal with it.

Teach your child to say "no" assertively by looking the person in the eye so that they know they really mean it and saying "No" with an assertive voice.

It is important for children to understand that they sometimes need to yell "NO" in an emergency. For example, if a stranger is trying to drag them into a car or if a friend is trying to throw them into deep water and they can't swim or somebody is trying to touch their private body parts. They need to yell "NO" as loud as they possibly can to draw the attention of adults around them.

Be aware that there may be circumstances under which your child may be too afraid to say no because they are being threatened or coerced. It is very important that they are reassured that it is not their fault, they can talk with you about anything and you will understand and support them no matter what has happened.

If children have had to use an assertive 'no' or emergency 'no' they need to tell someone on their Network.

Role play with your child: say "no" to them sheepishly, shyly (looking at the ground) or giggling and ask them if they think you are serious about saying no. This helps illustrate the importance of saying "no" assertively.

Practice yelling "NO!" for an emergency. Go outside and have your child yell "NO!" as loud as they can. Pretend that you are a stranger trying to get them into your car. Use whatever manipulations such a person would use, see if your child can attract the attention of others who could assist them.

Cyber Safety

The internet provides an opportunity for children to interact and learn on a global scale, and can be a wonderful learning tool. However, the internet also provides complete strangers with a direct link into your home, and into your child's life. The danger of this cannot be underestimated, so you need to educate yourself and your family about the potential dangers, and know what to do when faced with them.

Some simple strategies can be implemented, including setting strict rules for usage and regular supervision in order to ensure the rules are being adhered to:

- Have the computer set up in a family area so it must be used openly.
- Set time limits and identify sites permitted for visiting depending on the age of your child. Have it written down so you are both clear on which sites are allowed.
- Reinforce using the Three Safety Questions whilst online.
- Encourage your child to use an anonymous online name which is not gender specific.
- Make sure your child understands that his or her actual address is not to be given to anyone at all over the internet.
- Be vigilant about your child only using webcam when under supervision.
- Discourage the use of headphones for private conversations.
- Talk to your child about strangers online. Children need to understand that people online may not always be who they claim to be and speaking with them online is like speaking to a stranger on the street.
- Teach your child not to open mail from unknown sources.
- Encourage your child to come to you if they encounter any inappropriate or disturbing content that makes them feel unsafe.
- Have your computer password protected with each child as an individual user and yourself as the Administrator. This will allow you to monitor sites visited and restrict the sites accessible according to age.
- Type your child's name into Google. This will show you links that are connected to your child, and can in some instances let you see what other people are saying about him or her, or photos that have been taken of them, particularly on the social network site facebook.
- Be your child's friend on facebook.
- Have an open discussion with your child about private pictures.

- Have a family rule that all mobile phones will be put in a public place after a certain time at night, there is no reason for children to have phones in their bedrooms late at night.
- Have your child enter into a Cyber Agreement, copy below.

For further information visit www.netalert.gov.au or www.thinkuknow.org.au

Cyber Agreement

☐ I will never give out personal, private information such as my name, address – including country or state, age, banking information, phone number, sports team I play for, school I attend, sports or recreation clubs I am a member of, or any other personal information that could be used to identify me or help locate me.

☐ I will never give out information that will indentify other members of my family, nor give out information about the type of family I have.

☐ I will always use a nickname that does not reveal my identity, location or gender.

☐ I will never send my picture without checking with my parent/caregiver first.

☐ I will never open an email unless I know it is from somebody I trust.

☐ I will always tell my parent/caregiver if I come across anything that makes me feel uncomfortable, private pictures or gives me my Early Warning Signs.

☐ I will never agree to meet somebody without checking with a parent/caregiver first. If the parent/caregiver agrees, I will only meet them, with my parent/caregiver, in a public place, and I understand that this would be a rare occurrence.

☐ I will always gain permission from my parent/caregiver before exploring a new site.

☐ I will always speak openly with someone on my Network about any problems I have about the Internet, even if I have broken this agreement, because I know I can talk with someone about anything.

☐ I understand that this agreement applies whenever I access the Internet on any computer anywhere including school, internet cafes and friends' houses, and at any time of the day or night.

Name _____   Parent/Caregiver _____

Signature _____   Signature _____

Date _____   Date _____

© Copyright 2012 safe4kids **26**

Other things to consider:

- Make time each day to talk to your child about their day, how they are feeling and about things that matter to them.

- Teach your child to talk about their feelings with "I" statements; eg, "I feel...when...because..." Model this language yourself.

- Teach your child to monitor their own behaviours to do the right or safe thing, if they still insist on making a bad choice then there should be consequences. Discuss the consequences before the bad choice has occurred, a child should know what they are up for if they do something wrong or silly.

- If you are riding in the car to events, develop an action plan for different scenarios by playing games such as, "What could you do to keep yourself safe even if ..." "What could you do to keep yourself safe even if ... you were lost at the Show?"

- Be cautious with whom you entrust the care of your child; eg, babysitters, sport coaches, youth leaders, neighbours, friends parents etc. Be aware of whose house your child is sleeping over at and do what you have to do to make sure they will be properly supervised.

- Find out if there is a Protective Behaviours program taught at your child's school. Find out which day it is scheduled for and what the content is so you can discuss any issues or answer any questions your child may have.

- Reinforce Theme 1. For example, when disciplining your child, rather than telling them "don't do that" or "get down from there" ask them if they are being safe or unsafe, try and help them make the right choice. If they make a bad choice then you can use; "Now I'm getting my Early Warning Signs, I'm asking you to get down from there/stop the behaviour."

- Help your child to feel empowered, this will help make them less vulnerable to being bullied and less likely to give in to any form of abuse – physical, emotional, sexual or neglect.

- Although this book has focused on teaching your child, keep in mind the importance of practicing Protective Behaviours yourself, such as having your own Network and speaking with people about your feelings.

- Discuss what your children may see on the news. Debrief them so that they are not anxious. These teachable moments are priceless and once they have passed are hard to recoup.

Receiving a Disclosure

If your child discloses that they have been abused, either physically, sexually or emotionally, here are some suggestions which may help your child, and you, to feel safe:

1. Stay calm

Try to put your feelings aside as an outraged reaction will only reinforce your child's reluctance to disclose, and may make them think they have done something wrong.

2. Believe your child

Children rarely lie about abuse but they are often discouraged from disclosing because they think no-one will believe them. It is therefore very important they know that you believe them.

3. Offer reassurance

Reassure your child that it is not their fault and they haven't done anything wrong, they are not to blame. Use phrases such as; "I'm really pleased you told me." "You've done the right thing by telling someone on your Network." "I'm sorry this has happened to you but we'll work this out together."

4. Do not interrogate

Do not pressure your child to give in-depth details, they may have to repeat their story for authorities and they may find it distressing each time they have to recount the abuse.

Do not approach the perpetrator yourself, leave this to the authorities.

5. Make no promises

Do not promise to keep this a secret, use Protective Behaviours language to explain that you may have to tell someone on your Network.

6. Contact authorities:

The Department for Child Protection

Police Child Protection Unit.

Crimestoppers

- **Other contacts (Australia only):**

Kids Helpline 1800 551 800 or www.kidshelpline.com.au

NetAlert www.netalert.gov.au

Think U Know www.thinkuknow.org.au

The following pages have been left intentionally blank for colouring/notes.

Printed in Great Britain
by Amazon